My bounty is as boundless as the sea,

My love as deep; the more I give to thee,

The more I have, for both are infinite.

SHAKESPEARE, *ROMEO AND JULIET*

WEDDING

rings

WEDDING

rings

OSNAT GAD

WITH JO SCAMMATO

PHOTOGRAPHS BY ZEVA OELBAUM

STEWART, TABORI & CHANG · NEW YORK

To my husband, Larry, and my son, Derek, with love

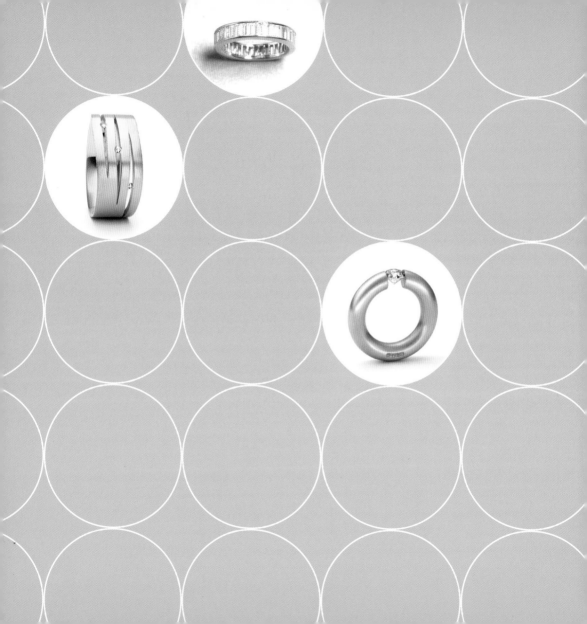

CONTENTS

DURING THE PAST TWENTY YEARS OF MY CAREER IN THE jewelry industry, working with gems and designing wedding rings, I have met many couples in love, who are starting their lives together. I know how important it is to make a perfect wedding ring for them. As they gaze at their chosen rings, I sense their overwhelming emotions at the prospect of their future.

The importance of the moment when the ring is placed on the finger is as precious as the ring itself. No matter what material the wedding ring is made of, its real value is measured in the love given between two people and their commitment to each other.

When wedding rings are placed on our fingers, never to be taken off, we know a new family has been created. The ring symbolizes the continuity and tradition of our past and it is forever connected to our cultures. Many rings remain in families for generations. When I asked my friends and family to allow us to take photos of their family wedding rings for this book, my sister gave us my grandmother's betrothal ring, which has been in our family since the late-nineteenth century. When I saw the ring again after many years, I felt a wonderful connection to my mother and grandmother. It was my mother who instilled in me an appreciation of the romance between a man and a woman through her love for my father. Many couples and families inspired me to research and share the romantic stories that make up this history of wedding rings.

Whether you use this book to help select your own wedding ring, give it as a gift to a newly engaged friend, share it with your partner when renewing your vows, or simply explore a timeless tradition, I hope you will enjoy learning about the rich history of wedding rings as much as I have. ○

Diamonds and a ruby grace this betrothal ring set in 20-carat gold that was ○ given to my grandmother on her engagement in Afghanistan in the nineteenth century. Diamonds were set in many of the betrothal rings among European couples in that period, and rubies were used because they symbolized the color of the heart. It was a surprise to me that in such a remote land, traditional betrothal rings were being used as a token of love.

TYING THE KNOT AND THE FIRST CIRCLES OF LOVE

With this ring I thee wed,
with my body I thee worship,
and with all my worldly goods,
I thee endow.

THE FIRST BOOK OF COMMON PRAYER

GETTING MARRIED IS COMMONLY REFERRED TO AS "tying the knot," but you might be surprised that our earliest ancestors literally tied the knot. They believed that a rope tied around various parts of the body could keep the soul from escaping, so when a caveman chose his mate, he brought her spirit under his control by tying cords made of braided grass around her wrists, ankles, and waist. Later, just the wrists were tied. Ultimately, the finger became the only part of the body to be encircled with grass or a lock of hair to symbolize the union of two lives. These first rings were formed out of rush, a hollowstemmed grass.

These rings, by Dutch designer Carla Nuis, are cast in silver and white gold from wax imprints. This solid print ring, intended for a man, is the reverse impression of the open version (see page 133), intended for a woman.
Photo: Eddy Wenting

The first known exchange of rings as objects of love took place in Egypt, around 2800 B.C. The pharaohs of Egypt regarded the circle as a symbol of eternity and believed the ring was a heavenly symbol that life and happiness and love had no beginning and no end. In modern Egypt some women still wear gold or silver ankle bracelets (known as *khulkhall*) to show that they are married.

Jewelry, regarded as highly symbolic of human emotion, was often found in the tombs of Egyptian mummies. When the tombs were rediscovered rings were found on the third finger of the left hand of the preserved bodies. The notion that a vein in this finger, *vena amoris*, leads directly to the heart has its roots in these ancient tombs. The earliest Egyptian rings were made of a single silver wire and later of single gold wires threaded together and knotted to hold a bezel. Gold was used because it was considered by the Egyptians as the substance of the sun, the flesh of the gods, who were associated with eternity.

o Sumerian cloisonné ring ca. 3000 B.C.E.; Louvre, Paris Réunion des Musées Nationaux/Art Resource, New York

The promise of eternal love and commitment between two people took hold very early on in the history of the human race and endures to this day. Everyone who wears and cherishes a wedding ring is continuing a tradition that spans the globe and thousands of years.

The first mention in Roman literature of a ring as a pledge of love is by Plautus, (254–184 B.C.). Marriage rings given at the time of betrothal, or what we now call the engagement, began in Rome in the second century B.C. According to Pliny (237–79? B.C.), a Roman writer and the foremost authority in ancient Europe, the bridegroom gave the bride first a gold ring to wear during the ceremony and at special events and later an iron ring to wear indoors.

Saint Clement of Alexandria (150?–215 A.D.), a Greek theologian who is considered the early Father of the Christian Church as a leader of the catechetical school at Alexandria, declared that the ring was not bestowed upon the prospective spouse as an ornament, but as proof that she might seal up whatever was worthy of special care in the household.

Many rings were found at Pompeii, in the house of Diomed, several of gold, which are believed to be wedding rings. One of the

One marriage custom of Ancient Rome was to give the betrothal ring to the bride on the point of a sword.

rings, featuring a man and woman joining hands, bears a resemblance to what would later be called the fede ring.

The marriage ceremony was regarded by the Jews in the first and second centuries as a contract between a young man and a woman of "full age." Males in the last day of their thirteenth year, and women in the second half of their eleventh year, were considered of marrying age and wed at their own will. For the Romans as well as Jews, the ring was intended as "earnest money," symbolizing the groom's promise that he had the means to support his bride-to-be.

Many magnificent works of art pay homage to the importance and symbolism of the wedding ring. In Venice, one of the world's most romantic cities, paintings by the great artist Tintoretto (1518–1594) adorn the walls of the Doges Palace. One of the paintings, completed in 1578, depicts the marriage of Bacchus and Ariadne being performed by Venus. The painting depicts the moment when Bacchus extends the hand holding a gold ring, preparing to place it on the left ring finger of Ariadne. Many couples on their honeymoon in Venice have been thrilled by the emotion conveyed in this painting.

○ Gold marriage ring inscribed with the names Dromascius and Betta, Merovingian, late 6th to 7th century A.D. Diameter, 1 in. (2.5 cm); Weight 0.8 oz. (24 g). The British Museum, London © Copyright The Trustees of the British Museum

As goldsmithing techniques improved more elaborate wedding bands were created. A ring believed to have originated in Roman Britain during the fourth century features beautiful open work, with sixteen rectangular panels containing intertwined geometric motifs. This type of design is known as *opus interasile* and required great skill on the part of the jewelry maker. The romantic message inserted into the leaf-like decoration and inscribed in sixteen central rectangles of the ring is "Ptolemios love charm." The strength and intensity of the gold reinforces the power of this token of love.

Another of the great achievements in jewelry was the art of the Celts in the Roman Empire. Personal ornaments in gold or less valuable metals were made with great technical skill, and featured filigree or granulation inlaid with garnets, colored glass, or enamel. Floral and leaf designs, along with intricate animal and human figures, also characterize jewelry of the Hellenistic Age and the Etruscan Era. Many of these motifs found their way onto wedding rings of that time.

○ Gold ring with Greek inscription "The love token of Polemios," 2nd-3rd century A.D. Diameter, 0.9 in. (2.2 cm). The British Museum, London, © Copyright The Trustees of The British Museum

From the fourth century on, as Christianity spread throughout Western Europe and its influence expanded, the wedding ring became symbolic of spouses' unity with Christ. Sometimes the betrothal and marriage took place on the same day and the betrothal ring also served as the wedding ring.

The Romans introduced the betrothal ring to the ancient Germans. The laws of the Goths, written in 643 A.D., declared, "Since there are many, who, forgetful of the plighted faith, defer the fulfillment of their nuptial contracts, this license should be suppressed." The laws also stated that when a declaration of marriage was made in the presence of a witness and the ring was given and accepted as "earnest money," the marriage ceremony must follow.

By 860 A.D. in Rome, the betrothal and the marriage ceremony were separate events according to an account by Pope Nicholas I. The bridegroom presented one ring at the betrothal and another for the wedding in the church. This is where the tradition of separate engagement and wedding rings was born, a practice which has lasted to this day. The etiquette of the time decreed that if the man decided not to marry his betrothed, the woman could keep the

To she who excels not only in virtue and prudence, but also in wisdom.

INSCRIPTION, ORIGINALLY IN GREEK, ON A GOLD RING FROM THE FOURTH CENTURY, B.C.

betrothal ring. However, if she changed her mind, she was expected to return it.

Joining the hands through a round object was (and of course still is) considered essential to the wedding ritual. If a bridegroom could not afford a ring for his bride, a bracelet, a curtain ring, or even the church's key ring was used in the Christian ceremony. In the fourth century Saint Augustine wrote, "No priest shall hesitate to wed a couple who present themselves before the altar, if the bride and bridegroom are not able because of poverty, to give rings to each other; for the offering of the earnest money is a matter of decorum, not of necessity." Substituting a round object for the wedding ring was common in Iceland and the Orkney Islands north of Scotland as late as the eighteenth century.

Then on my finger
I'll have a ring
Not one of rush,
but a golden thing;
And I shall be glad
as a bird in spring,
Because I am married
o' Sunday.

OLD ENGLISH BALLAD

The Constitutions of Richard the Bishop of Salisbury, England, refer to the use of rush rings in England in 1217 for mock marriages. If a man placed a rush ring, or any ring of metal on a woman's hand—even in sport or jest—she was supposed to become friendly with him. During this time, an ecclesiastical court often made marriage the penalty for seduction with a false promise. In this case, a rush ring or ring made of straw would be used at the ceremony.

Ring soon destined to encircle the finger of a beauteous girl, a ring having no worth except the love of the giver.

PLAUTUS,
MILES GLORIOUS

SIGNET, FEDE, GIMMEL, CLADDAGH, AND POSEY RINGS

I am a token of love,
do not throw me away.

INSCRIPTION ORIGINALLY IN LATIN
ON THE BACK OF A THIRTEENTH—
CENTURY FEDE RING

DURING ROMAN BRITAIN, SIGNET RINGS WERE AMONG the most common betrothal rings. Signet rings feature an image engraved in the metal or directly on the gemstone and represent a man's signature. These rings were first used by the Greeks, and they gave another person authority to act in his name. By placing his signet ring on a woman's finger, a man promised his future wife equal authority in his household and entrusted her with his wealth. The emotional bonding of marriage, the couple's faith in their future, and the shared commitment to create a loving family and happy home are all embodied in the ring. A pledge similar to that of a signet ring was symbolized by little keys that were attached to some wedding rings.

The Takohl Treasure Ring®, a contemporary interpretation of the gimmel ring, ○ presents a simple band. But a hidden latch opens to reveal a secret inscription or precious gems; designed by Tammy Kohl for Takhol Design, with a matching engagement ring.

o Gold signet ring,
English, 16th century;
Victoria & Albert
Museum, London/Art
Resource, NY

o Silver Bavarian
marriage ring with
lock and key pendants,
symbolic of the
responsibility and
control a wife is given
in the partnership of
matrimony. South
Germany (Bavaria),
19th century;
The Alice and Louis
Koch Collection.

In this fede ring, the use  of sapphire, symbolic of fidelity, in conjuction with the heart shape indicates its use as a betrothal or wedding ring. The inscription of the Roman numeral "XX" possibly had a personal meaning, while the "pea pod ornament" visible on the back of the ring bezel points to the date of the ring. West European, ca. 1620–50; The Alice and Louis Koch Collection.

Amor vincit omnia (love conquers all)

POSY INSCRIPTION

"He gives a gold ring," said Saint Clement, "not for ornament, but that she may with it seal up what has to be kept safe, as the care of keeping the house belongs to her."

Rings with two hands firmly clasped together or placed one on top of the other were often worn as betrothal rings or occasionally as tokens of affection. The joined hands, etched in gold, or engraved on gemstones, symbolized spiritual unity and commitment to family. By the nineteenth century, these rings were still popular and ring collectors gave them the name fede rings, from the old Italian *mani in fede* which means "hands in faith." Fede rings are still used in rural parts of Normandy and in Galway. Mothers often hand them down to their oldest daughters.

During the Renaissance, a time of romance in all aspects of life and art, jewelers were inspired to create a ring that beautifully represented the joining of two lives. The gimmel ring (from the Latin word for twins, *gemelli*) was actually two (or sometimes three) separate rings that joined together to appear as one ring. Most gimmel rings consisted of two interlacing hoops that only a jeweler

○ Gimmel fede ring, gold cast, chased and enameled; German; 16th century; V & A Images, The Victoria and Albert Museum, London

could separate and rejoin. The future bride and groom each wore half of the ring until their marriage, when both rings were placed on the bride. Imagine their excitement at the wedding when the separate rings were united into one, truly symbolizing the union of their hearts.

Gimmel rings often contained hidden inscriptions. Gemstones sometimes decorated the gimmel rings, and a ruby and diamond set in a heart signified the promise of passion and permanence, qualities essential to a successful marriage both then and now.

A contemporary interpretation of the beloved gimmel ring was created by the American jeweler Takhol and award-winning designer Tammy Kohl. A simple band is seen from the outside but a hidden latch contains the treasure—either a secret inscription or precious gems. A matching engagement ring is also available, and it too contains hidden treasures (see page 26).

My love is fixed;
I will not range
I like my choice too
well to change.

OLD POESY
INSCRIPTION

As if a piece of precious metal formed into a circle weren't enough to commemorate love, the addition of personal messages inside the wedding ring captivated many couples. Adding sweet words of devotion to the ring made it even more special and unique.

Wedding rings contained inscriptions as far back as the fourth century B.C. A gold Greek betrothal ring from this time bears the inscription, "To her who excels not only in virtue and prudence, but also in wisdom." Another ring bears the single word "honey" and one has a message any bride would love to receive: "I rejoice in the gift because of the affection of giver."

In love at night
is my delight

INSCRIPTION

These rings are known as posy rings (from the word poesy or poetry). They were sometimes called gypsy rings because they were sold by gypsies or middle-European bohemians. The French called them *chanson*, meaning "song." Whatever names these rings have been given throughout the ages, they have always inspired the hearts of couples in love, from the Middle Ages to modern times. The inscriptions were often in rhyme and were usually in French because it was considered the language of love. How wonderful to gaze at your wedding ring, knowing that the precious metal next to your skin describes the emotions in your partner's soul. On marriage rings, these sweet messages of love were engraved on the outside, proudly displayed for all to view. Rings between lovers, however, were inscribed on the inside to keep their sentiments a secret.

O Gold posy ring, inscribed, "Many are the stars I see, but in my eye no star like thee." England, 18th century A.D. Diameter, 0.6 in. (1.5 cm). The British Museum, London © Copyright The Trustees of The British Museum

The people of West Connemara in Ireland used claddagh rings, which have hands holding a crowned heart. The use of images of hands make these reminiscent of the fede rings of earlier times. Cartier in Paris and some sophisticated London jewelers made expensive versions of this motif, like an engagement ring made with two hearts, one was a ruby with diamonds.

During the seventeenth and eighteenth centuries—the Age of Enlightenment—there were many innovations in politics, changes in society, and technical advances in craftsmanship. These changes were soon reflected in engagement and wedding rings, which included the imaginative use of Cupid's bow and arrow or turtledoves. In ballrooms and salons, which were still lit by candles, these precious objects looked even more splendid and received a wealth of attention and compliments.

Garlands, bows, and pairs of hearts began to adorn love and marriage rings. These romantic motifs appealed to the new masters of jewelry design like Peter Carl Fabergé and Louis-François Cartier. The emotions that drew a couple to "tie a bow" around their lives and join two hearts into one were perfectly manifested in precious metals. These rings were made exceptionally beautiful by the use of green, pink, and white gold, in addition to the traditional yellow.

O Gold and pearl "anelli chianini" were marriage rings worn in the Valdechiana region near Arezzo. Their dimensions depended very much on the wealth of the family, and variations existed with different stones. Italian (Arezzo), 19th century. The Alice and Louis Koch Collection.

According to Irish tradition, when a claddagh ring is worn with the hands holding O the crown pointed toward the fingertip, the wearer is in love or married. When worn in the opposite direction it indicates the wearer is unattached. Claddagh wedding rings represent the traditions of the people of West Connemara, Ireland.

RINGS AROUND THE WORLD: CUSTOMS, RITUALS, AND FAITHS

Now you will feel no rain,
for each of you will be shelter for the other.
Now you will feel no cold,
for each of you will be warmth for the other.
Now there is no more loneliness;
now you are two persons but there is only
one life before you.

APACHE MARRIAGE BLESSING

THE WEDDING RING AS THE PHYSICAL EMBLEM OF THE
emotional bond between lovers has prevailed throughout the centuries
and in all parts of the world. Each culture has adapted the use of the
ring to its own customs and beliefs, adding new chapters to the history
of this timeless circle of love.

One longstanding tradition is that the wedding ring is worn on the
third finger of the left hand. You might wonder why this is the case.
The custom is actually so common today that this finger is known as

Life Crest Love Rings in platinum, hand engraved with life crest animals, ○
are inspired by the legends of Northwest Coast Indians;
Bill Helin, Tsimshian Indian Artist.

the ring finger. As mentioned in Chapter One, the Egyptians believed that the vein from the third finger of the left hand ran directly to the heart. Another reason for the ring being worn on the third finger is that in many church weddings, the priest touched the fingers of the bride's left hand beginning with the index finger, as he evoked the names of the Father, the Son and the Holy Ghost. He then placed the ring on the last finger he touched.

But as customary as this placement seems today, it wasn't always so. Rituals for the blessing of the ring and placing it on the finger of the bride can be traced back to the eleventh century. It appears it was usual to place the ring on the right hand of the bride. This is shown in nearly all depictions of marriages from the thirteenth to sixteenth centuries.

Customs have definitely varied from place to place in the past. For example, in France, from the eleventh to fifteenth century, the wedding ring was placed on the middle finger of the right hand of the bride, but in the diocese of Liege, a French province bordering Belgium, it was placed on the third finger of the right hand.

...for whither thou goest,
I will go
and where thou lodgest,
I will lodge
thy people shall be
my people
and thy God my God.

RUTH 1:16–18

One of Ghirlandrajo's frescoes in the church of Santa Croce, in Florence, depicts the betrothal of the Virgin. The ring is placed by Joseph on the third finger of the Virgin's right hand. The Italian Renaissance painter, Raphael, who is considered one of the greatest and most popular artists of all time, was impressed with the beautiful tradition of the betrothal ring and featured it in his famous painting, *Le Sposalizio*, which translates as "Marriage of the Virgin." The painting shows Mary and Joseph in the center facing each other. Between them is the high priest, who is bringing their right hands toward each other. Joseph, with his right hand, is placing the ring on the third finger of the right hand of the Virgin.

Dearly beloved: We have come together in the presence of God to witness and bless the joining together of this man and this woman in Holy Matrimony.

EPISCOPAL NUPTIAL BLESSING

The practice of placing the ring on the third finger of the left hand first appears in writing in the Book of Common Prayer of Edward VI from 1549. The reason for the change of hand is not known, but Isidor of

O If a traditional engagement ring is forgone a round diamond eternity wedding ring, set invisibly from all sides for maximum sparkle, in platinum is a good option for the wedding band.

41

Seville in the early part of the seventh century followed the writings of Aulus Gellius, a Roman essayist from the first century, who wrote that the vein flowing to the heart was from the left hand and not the right hand as many believed at the time. The change in English usage was followed in 1614. However this alteration was not observed by English Catholics until the middle of the eighteenth century.

No matter what finger the wedding ring is worn on—and even if it is not placed on a finger at all—it still represents romantic love. Each culture interprets the placement of the ring in its own way but the notion of eternal love remains universal.

Some Greek women wear their rings on their left hand while engaged and on the right hand after marriage. During the marriage ceremony, the priest places the wedding rings on the third finger of the bride's and groom's right hand. Then the couple exchanges the rings.

In southern Germany today, men and women wear their wedding rings on the fourth finger of the left hand. However it is worn on the right in northern Germany.

Wedding rings were sometimes worn on rosaries, according to a passage in the will of Ann Barrett from the sixteenth century. Mingling the concepts of marital love and devotion to a higher divine love helped seal the bonds more securely.

I take you as my husband. I promise to be true to you in good times and bad, in sickness and in health. I will love you and honor you all the days of my life.

ROMAN CATHOLIC VOW

A bride, in order to be happy, should step over the church threshold with her right foot.

SUPERSTITION

The baguette cut is a method of cutting diamonds in the shape of a long narrow rectangle bordered by four step-cut facets. This diamond ring is set vertically in 18-carat yellow gold between two parallel bands of metal in a channel setting.

42

On the day of the death of Queen Louisa of Prussia, her husband, King Friedrich Wilhelm III, prepared a list of the rings she was wearing. It includes the notation, "Our betrothal ring, on the little finger of the right hand." During the reign from 1714 to 1727 of George I of England, wearing the marriage ring on the thumb became popular.

Today in India, a wedding ring, made of gold and about an inch wide, is often worn on the thumb. It may be worn only during the days celebrating the wedding ceremony or, occasionally, for six to twelve months after the wedding. Then the gold is melted down to be made into another piece of jewelry.

In the Jewish marriage ritual of the seventh and eighth centuries, the bridegroom placed the wedding ring—a plain gold band—on the middle finger of the bride's right hand. Jewish law, as stated in the Talmud, requires the wedding ring to belong to the groom and to be of solid metal, with no gems adorning it. In the wedding ceremony—called Kidushin—the union of the couple is also a union with God in a state of holiness. The simple, unbroken band is used to maintain the sacredness of the marriage, without material distractions. This practice continues in many ceremonies today, so Jewish couples often use the simple band when they take their vows, but may add another more elaborate wedding ring later.

Behold you are consecrated unto me with this ring, according to the law of Moses and Israel.

JEWISH WEDDING VOW

○ Wedding rings, Italian, 16th/17th century. Enamel on gold. Musée du Judaisme, Paris, Photo by J.G. Berizzi. Réunion des Musées Nationaux/Art Resource, NY

In contrast to the simple bands used in Jewish weddings of earlier times, Jewish wedding rings in sixteenth and seventeenth centuries Venice and southern Germany were richly enameled, often made of gold filigree and elaborately decorated. Those wide bands were topped with three-dimensional miniature gabled houses or synagogues with high roofs and miniature gates that open toward heaven.

One ring from that era features the figures of Adam and Eve in Paradise, surrounded by animals. Another includes a reproduction of Solomon's Temple. Most Jewish wedding rings were inscribed with the Hebrew words "Mazel Tov," meaning "good luck." During the wedding ceremony, the groom placed the ring on the middle finger of the bride's right hand. After the wedding, the ring was removed from the bride's hand and kept by one of the families or by the congregation.

A finger ring made of onyx is said to have been worn by the Virgin Mary at her marriage to Joseph. Since 1472, it has been kept in a cathedral in Perugia, Italy, suspended from a jeweled crown that hangs in a gilded silver tabernacle. Since the sixteenth century, nuns have received a plain yellow gold band upon taking vows of chastity, poverty, and service. Few bore inscriptions, but one found from the 1300s is engraved with the words, "With this ring of chastity, I am espoused to Jesus Christ."

In ancient China, the ring was regarded as a complete circle, combining and containing every divine principle. Like the Egyptians, the Chinese saw the ring as an everlasting and unbroken circle, without beginning or end. Among the many ladies in the courts of ancient China, the emperor's favorite woman was required to wear a silver ring. If she presented the emperor with a descendant, she received the gift of a gold ring, which she wore on her left hand.

In the marriage ritual of the Greek Church, the groom gave the bride a wedding ring, a pair of shoes, and a kiss. The ring and the shoes served as symbols of securing the lady's hands and feet, while the kiss was intended to forever seal the secrets between husband and wife.

In an old custom in the Russian branch of the Eastern Church, the bride's wedding ring was made of silver and the groom's of gold to indicate that he was superior to her. Of course modern brides do not stand for this inequality, and so today they are also given gold rings. Another custom in Russia was for the husband to wear his wedding ring on his forefinger.

> I give this ring to you, my beloved, my friend, my wife.
>
> UNITED CHURCH OF CHRIST VOW

Some Greek and Russian churches still practice "crowning." During the betrothal ceremony wedding rings are exchanged and a binding marriage contract is signed. At the nuptial ceremony, held later, a crown of garland wreaths and vines wrapped in silver or gold, or even a crown made in precious metal and decorated with gemstones, is placed on the heads of the bride and groom by the priest or the best man. This is when the marriage is officially—and divinely—sanctioned. The crown remains with the couple for life and sometimes it is buried with the husband or wife.

In Southern India, Tamil grooms place the wedding ring on the middle toe of the bride's right foot. For ordinary people, the wedding ring for the toe is made of silver because gold is considered too precious for the feet. However, royals get married with gold toe rings. The groom leads his new wife on a walk of seven paces as a fire blazes before them. He then places a symbol of fertility—the bindior—in the middle of her forehead and finishes the ritual by hanging a pendant, held by a silk cord around her neck. She will wear this emblem of marriage until her husband dies.

In the Middle Ages, a man often kept a betrothal ring suspended from the band of his hat to tease all the maidens. Wedding rings

I am the word and you are the melody. I am the melody and you are the word.

TRADITIONAL
HINDU MANTRA

Silver toe rings–traditionally worn in pairs–are used in certain **O** Indian wedding ceremonies.

engraved with fruit, orange blossoms, and wreaths recall a tradition begun during the First Crusade, when the groom placed a wreath of orange blossoms on the bride's head as a blessing. The orange tree is evergreen and is the only tree that bears fruit and blossoms at the same time. In China, the white blossoms are symbols of innocence, chastity, and purity, worn by the bride to enhance her fertility. What a beautiful image to evoke on the wedding day.

Muslim men in Saudi Arabia do not wear gold as it is considered a sign of wealth and power that is not consistent with the Islamic religion's emphasis on equality, humility and purity. Therefore, when they wear wedding rings, they are of silver or platinum. Women, however, are permitted to wear gold, and it is a long-standing custom for grooms to give their future wives gifts of gold jewelry or even gold coins when they propose marriage.

At weddings in Tunis, the Arabs custom is for the groom to place the wedding ring on the first finger of the bride's left hand. On this occasion, her finger- and toe-nails are stained a deep red with henna as are her eyebrows to form a single bar over the eyes, in keeping with the customs of the land. To avoid the "evil eye," the couple's home is protected by a pair of gilded horns set above the door along with a favorite charm.

I pledge, in honesty and with sincerity, to be for you an obedient and faithful wife.

I pledge, in honesty and sincerity, to be for you a faithful and helpful husband.

MUSLIM WEDDING VOW

50

tying the knot

A wedding ring adorned with a Heracles knot—a symbol of fidelity in marriage—was found in Alexandria in about 300 B.C. The Heracles knot was a device used to tie a bride's garment, which was then untied by the groom during the marriage ceremony.

In one Hebrew betrothal ritual, a ring made of three bands joined together was separated into three parts over a bible when the couple became engaged. One circle went to the woman, another to the man, and the third to a witness. The witness escorted the pair to the ceremony where the bride put on all three rings, which were reunited on her finger.

In India, when the Hindu groom secured a ribbon around the throat of his bride, their marriage was considered legal and binding.

○ Widespread during the Hellenistic period, the Heracles knot is symbolic of fidelity. The proportions and delicacy of this gold ring suggest its date. 2nd-1st century B.C. The Alice and Louis Koch Collection

Around the world, the use of the wedding ring in the marriage ceremony has been enhanced by different ethnic and cultural beliefs. The enchanting circle of love has circled the globe while retaining its eternal magic.

Today in the Greek Church, the priest places a ring on the fourth finger of each partner's left hand. Then they proceed to exchange them. In Portugal, the hands of the bride and groom are tied together by the

priest's stole at the marriage ceremony. Then the ring is placed on the bride's finger. In France and French-speaking countries, many wedding rings consist of three rings interwoven and flowing together. They stand for faith, hope and love. In Africa today some wedding rituals include the binding of the bride and groom's wrists together with braided grass. African slaves, who were forbidden to marry, "Jumped the Broom," to make public their love for one another. This tradition is still performed today by African Americans at marriage ceremonies in remembrance of their past. Scandinavian women may wear three rings: one for engagement, one for marriage and one for motherhood.

Wedding rings are the most personal gifts between people in love. Yet, each is a link in the unbroken chain of the history of romance and commitment throughout the world.

Lucky is the bride who sees a toad, spider, dove, or lamb on her way to church.

SUPERSTITION

O Gold Wedding ring with mill grain resembling the ancient art of granulation, an Etruscan gold-working technique, revived in the 19th century, in which minute grains of gold are applied to a metal surface forming patterns in low relief.

SPARKLING DIAMONDS AND RAINBOWS OF GEMS

Slowly a gem forms, in the ancient, once more molten rocks
Of two human hearts, two ancient rocks, a man's heart and a woman's
That is the crystal of peace, the slow hard jewel of trust,
The sapphire of fidelity
The gem of mutual peace emerging from the wild chaos of love

D.H LAWRENCE, *FIDELITY*

A DIAMOND FIRST APPEARED IN A YELLOW GOLD BETROTHAL ring for European royalty at the end of the fifteenth century, given by Archduke Maximilian of Austria to his intended wife, Mary of Burgundy. The word diamond comes from *adamas*, a Greek word meaning "unconquerable."

Diamonds graced many of the betrothal rings among European royalty toward the end of the fifteenth century. The Venetians discovered that the diamond could be made exceptionally brilliant through fine polishing and recognized its value as the hardest,

A wide diamond ring in 18-carat white gold, designed in a pattern of half moons ○ with bezel diamonds between them; designed by Alessandra for OGI.

56

most enduring substance in nature—a perfect sign of constancy and permanence in marriage. Many of the engagement and wedding rings worn from the fifteenth through the eighteenth centuries were set with gems chosen for their beauty of color or their popularity. Garnets, amethysts, emeralds, and diamonds were used either as solitaires or combined with pearls.

In 1518 at the age of two, Princess Mary of England was betrothed to an infant, the Dauphin of France, to enhance the British throne's alliance with France. A gold engagement ring, set with a glittering diamond, was given to the future bride, sized for her tiny finger.

America's first First Lady, Martha Washington, was married in 1749 with a sparkling diamond wedding ring, to her first husband, Daniel Parke Curtis. The ring had a central diamond surrounded by six smaller stones. When Martha and George Washington married many years later with the same ring, a locket was added to hold a lock of George's hair.

A wealth of precious stones became available to European jewelry makers from the New World in the seventeenth century. Rings

And as this round
Is nowhere found
To flaw, or else to sever,
So let our love
As endless prove,
And pure as gold forever.

ROBERT HERRICK

○ Pave set round diamonds surround channel set square sapphires in an 18-carat white gold band that makes a lovely anniversary or wedding ring.

featured gemstones in symbolic colors—red ruby as the color of the heart, blue sapphire to evoke the heavens—but the diamond was the most desirable and majestic gem.

With the discovery in South Africa during the late nineteenth century of huge deposits of the spectacular, durable and precious diamond, the betrothal ring was reborn as a dazzling jewel every woman desired. Now, it was called the engagement ring. Though expensive, the diamond could be cut and set in a variety of styles and sizes, bringing it within the reach of almost every couple. The Dutch in South Africa discovered the new diamonds and the British dominated the industry in the early 1900s. However, it was the Americans of the 1900s who embraced diamonds with pride, affection, and esteem. Almost all diamond engagement rings of this period were round stones. A few were cut as ovals, and rings set in France were often a marquise cut. Most diamond rings were made with yellow gold, the diamond set inside a white gold bezel, allowing the white metal next to the diamond to surround it in white light. Large diamonds were reserved for necklaces, pendants, and tiaras, so the smaller stones were used for rings. These small stones were often surrounded by even more diamonds to make them appear larger.

This platinum wedding ring with rich red square rubies and round diamonds ○ (ca. 1930) follows the geometric, dazzlingly colorful forms of the Art Deco era.

At the beginning of the twentieth century, the magazine *Ladies Home Journal* gave the diamond engagement ring its blessing, saying it was in good taste whether worn during the day or evening.

A revolution began in the lavish creativity of jewelry-making at the end of World War I. It was the Art Deco era and jewelry followed the same linear, geometric, dazzlingly colorful and highly stylized forms that were found in art and architecture. Art Deco styles made wedding rings even more ornate and appealing. Diamonds were featured in delicate platinum settings, in shapes of exotic flowers and mythical animals. To this day, these creations inspire the taste of brides in choosing their wedding rings.

o An ornate wedding ring with diagonally bar-set baguette diamonds surrounded by brilliant pave diamonds (ca. 1915–40).

Gemstones are treasured for their beauty, rarity, and durability. Diamonds are highly prized for their fire and brilliancy; rubies, emeralds and sapphires for the intensity of their colors. Most natural gemstones vary in color, shade, or hue, due to the natural presence of finely dispersed particles of minerals. Because the same species of

the meaning of gemstones

DIAMONDS

Produced by thunderbolts, protected the wearer from disease and evil, and granted the wearer courage.

SAPPHIRES

Representing purity, the color of heaven, these dazzling blue stones protect the wearer against dark spirits, such as envy.

EMERALDS

These pure green gems are symbols of faithfulness, immortality and youth.

RUBIES

Rich and red, they are gems of the sun. Their fire always shines to guard the home and provide a life of peace and health.

stone may come in several colors, color alone is the least reliable means of identifying a gemstone and the quality of the color affects their value.

Stones also vary in the way they are cut to reflect light. When gemstones first became popular, the rose cut was favored. As their popularity increased in the late twentieth century, the brilliant, or round, cut became more common. Large rubies, sapphires, and

emeralds are often cut into cushion shapes, with many facets. The emerald cut is frequently used for diamonds. All of these stones represent highly concentrated monetary value, but they cannot always be accurately identified by sight alone. This is where the skill and talent of a gemologist comes in.

The promise of eternal connection was often literally spelled out on the wedding ring itself, as the gems were arranged by the first letters of their names: ruby, emerald, garnet, amethyst, ruby, and diamond for REGARD; lapis, opal, vermeil, and emerald for LOVE. Another favorite was DEAREST. The name of the loved one might also be spelled out in stones.

○ Silver-gilt ruby betrothal ring. The rubies, as well as the heart shape of the center stone, are symbolic of love. Western European, 1760. The Alice and Louis Koch Collection.

Sometimes the stones would be arranged in a form of a pansy flower called *pansee* in French, standing for "think of the giver." In one ring a flower head is placed between the fingers of a pair of hands created in the metal, adding extra dimension and charm. Sometimes the message of love was conveyed more directly by gem-set rings where the bezels were set with conjoined heart-shaped rubies and diamonds, perhaps surmounted by a knot or a bow. The fashion for these jewels reached a high point at the turn of the nineteenth century.

Three rings in platinum: princess-cut diamonds, and square cut sapphires ○ and rubies with hand engraving, are channel set all the way around the rings. A collection for each anniversary, they can be worn stacked on top of each other.

The seventeenth century was a time of the use of human hair in wedding rings, a true and permanent souvenir of the giver and a symbol of commitment through the ages. An openwork band of gold, currently in the Victoria and Albert Museum, is made to contain a lock of hair, which is decorated with brightly enameled lovebirds. It dates from about 1675.

Among the many fancy betrothal and wedding rings, some had perfume wells, such as one with a bouquet of stones set on a tiny hinge that opened to reveal a well for a few drops of perfume. These scented-engagement rings perfumed the fingers delicately and added to the pleasure when a lover kissed his lady's hand.

Queen Victoria (1819–1901) received a snake ring from Prince Albert, which was composed of fourteen hinged joints, set with diamonds. A crowned heart ring, whose origins are unknown, is set with diamonds held by two white enameled hands and inscribed, "Dudley and Katherine, united 26. Mar., 1706."

Marriage is an expression of faith in eternity and by the 1930s, many wedding rings featured stones, usually diamonds, all around the ring.

Called a jeweled hoop by some, this ring came to be known as the eternity ring and was worn instead of or in addition to a plain platinum or gold band.

The Duchess of Kent was married in 1934, wearing three eternity rings, one of rubies, one of diamonds, and one of sapphires—the colors of the British flag. An eternity ring made by Cartier had six diamonds, each the size of a pea, hanging from the hoop. The ring sparkled each time the hand moved, celebrating the richness and light of the loving marriage.

More than one-third of marriages today involve a bride or groom who has been married before. A woman's first wedding ring may have been traditional, plain metal or one with white diamonds. A second marriage offers the chance to be more adventurous, to have a wedding ring of rubies, emeralds, or sapphires—or perhaps one with colored diamonds.

Diamonds exhibit a wide range of transparency and color. Transparency is a measure of the amount of light that passes through a diamond rather than being absorbed. Structural imperfections or dislocations and the presence of trace elements, mainly nitrogen,

I marry you with my eyes wide open. You have helped me let go of the past and embrace the future. Thank you for making me laugh again. Bless you for taking my hand as I begin anew.

VOW IN A SECOND
MARRIAGE CEREMONY

cause color in diamond, resulting in a dazzling array of natural diamonds in green, blue, red, orange, yellow, pink, and brown. These stones are unique and gorgeous. Once reserved only for royalty, diamonds in all the colors of the rainbow—rare gifts from nature—can now be worn by anyone.

The chance to choose a new wedding ring is as exciting as the opportunity to find new love, a new life and to enjoy the emotions of marriage all over again.

○ Platinum gold engagement ring set with fancy color yellow diamond in the center, surrounded by two emerald-cut emeralds, and triangle diamonds. The ring was given to the author by her husband on their engagement. A matching platinum wedding ring set with intense yellow diamonds to match the color of the yellow center diamond.

OLD, NEW, BORROWED, BLUE—AND MORE

✤

Love him who gave thee this ring of gold,
'Tis he must kiss thee when thou art old.

INSCRIPTION ON A SEVENTEENTH-CENTURY
ENGLISH WEDDING BAND

ROMANTIC DESIGNS OF EARLIER CENTURIES NOW ENCHANT
brides of the twenty-first century. The simple beauty of engraved
orange blossoms is popular again. Inscriptions of names and dates and
the simple words, "with love," have a meaning to lovers today just as
they did in the past. Antique rings shine from the fingers of married
women who are delighted to celebrate their future with a treasure from
the past. Reputable antique shops and auction houses offer exquisite,
one-of-a-kind wedding rings imbued with a history of love.

By choosing an antique ring, or being married in her mother's
or grandmother's ring, a bride can satisfy the "something old" part of

Linked diamond rings in yellow gold resemble the gimmel ring which ⚬
separates into many interlinked parts; designed by Jytte Klove, Denmark.

"something old, something new, something borrowed, something blue." A sapphire or piece of turquoise jewelry can be the "something blue" part, in addition to the traditional garter tied with blue ribbon. Some brides may have their grandmothers' ring redesigned to be more modern while retaining the sentimental value of something passed down through generations. Platinum or white gold is often added to rings that were once simply yellow gold to make them more contemporary.

If a couple decides to marry on the spur of the moment while aboard a ship, or in some other unusual circumstance, with no time to find a wedding ring, a rubber band can be used. In fact a band of any material can seal the marriage contract, as long as it is round. The circle of love is sacred, regardless of its material.

The wedding ring played a unique role in the war between Germany and France in the nineteenth century. Many German women donated their gold wedding bands to the government to help pay the costs of battle. They proudly wore beautifully crafted wedding bands made of metal called Berlin ironwork, which was cast and lacquered black, and is now quite rare. These iron wedding rings were inscribed with the words "I gave gold for iron."

o Crafted by Ralph Bakker for the mother of his children, this gold ring was welded from old jewelry given to him by his mother and grandmother, 2000; photo by Ralph Bakker

71

○ The ring has three hoops that are put inside each other. The innermost one bears a hidden inscription, "Von dir geliebt zu sein. Das ist mein wunsch allein," meaning "To be loved by you. That is my only wish." Included are the initials of the couple and the date, 1826. German (Hesse), 1826. The Alice and Louis Koch Collection

Brides aren't always the only ones to enjoy rings of affection. Sometimes rings were simply gifts between lovers. Inscriptions and love poems such as *amo te*, which means "I love you" have been found in love rings from the story of Plautus (254–184 B.C.), a Roman comic dramatist, in his *Miles Gloriosus* to contemporary times.

Men often exchanged rings as tokens of close friendships with each other. The nineteenth century painter John Everett Mallais wrote to a friend, "I don't think I shall have the strength to say good bye. Scarcely a night passes but that I cry like an infant over the thought that I may not see you again. I wish I had something to remember you by and I desire that you should…get yourself a signet ring which you must as always wear…Get a good one and your initials engraved thereon."

This yellow gold wedding ring with subtle geometric ○ patterns of V's and X's is handcrafted.

At the Mechanic's Exhibition in Boston in 1841, a cake weighing 3,300 pounds was displayed. Baked inside were fifty gold rings! Visitors were invited to buy slices of the cake. How sweet to eat the tasty dessert and, if you were lucky, also receive a gold ring.

In a couple of instances, purchasing a piece of cake wasn't even necessary to get a ring—being a wedding guest was enough. In Persia, the bridegroom once gave a ring to everyone who attended the ceremony. Ladies present at the wedding of the future Louis XVI with the Archduchess Marie-Antoinette in 1770 were given rings with miniature portraits of the bride and groom as keepsakes. And at the marriage of Queen Victoria to Prince Albert, six dozen guests received rings as souvenirs, each one having a profile portrait of the bride engraved upon it, with the inscription, "Victoria Regina."

○ An Art Deco platinum diamond wedding ring has an intertwining pattern set with tapered baguette diamonds. The center diamonds in the pattern are set closely, so there is no space between the stones. Much time and attention was given to create this special ring. Both the jeweler and setter are master craftsmen practicing an old art that is vanishing today.

The guests weren't the only ones to receive gifts. Queen Victoria gave her bridesmaids jewels set entirely with blue turquoise, the color of the beautiful flower, the Forget Me Not. Turquoise was often used in wedding rings of the Victorian era to represent the flower's message of true, everlasting love.

Many brides gave their bridesmaids such gifts, symbolically asking to be remembered by their friends even though they were now married. The Tiffany & Company catalogue published in 1881 advised the bride to allow her attendants to keep the flowers they carried down the aisle and to give them a souvenir of the occasion such as a locket, pin, or bangle bracelet. The bridegroom was also told to give small gifts, usually of jewelry, to each of the bridesmaids in his wedding.

○ This jeweled eagle brooch made of gold, pearls and blue turquoise, the color of the flower, "Forget me not," was a gift given by Queen Victoria to her bridesmaids when she married Prince Albert. 1840; The British Museum, London, © Copyright the Trustees of the British Museum

Can a woman give a betrothal ring to a man? One strong-minded sixteenth century heroine did just that. In William Shakespeare's *The Merchant of Venice*, Portia gives Bassanio a ring and states that he should keep it forever:

> *I gave my love a ring and made him swear*
> *Never to part with it; and here he stands;*
> *I dare be sworn for him he would not leave*
> *nor pluck it from his finger, for the wealth*
> *That the world masters.*

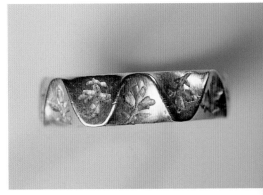

○ Gold posy ring bearing the inscription "loialte dort" which in a marriage ring could be interpreted as "loyalty endows." The oak leaves signify loyalty and constancy of friendship. English, 15th century. The Alice and Louis Koch Collection

Although it's been said that women are the more sentimental of the two sexes, Louis IX (Saint Louis) was so moved by the beauty of the ring used at his betrothal to Marguerite de Provence in 1231 that on his deathbed he asked that it be buried with his body.

FAMOUS DESIGNERS

To her who merits all my love

DEVELOPMENTS DURING THE INDUSTRIAL REVOLUTION
led to the mass production of many items, including wedding rings.
To maintain the distinction between the classical standards desired by
the aristocratic members of society and the commercialization of mass-
produced goods for the middle class, designer jewelry was born. Great
jewelry houses like Cartier and Boucheron in Paris, Garrard in London,
Faberge in Russia, and Tiffany in New York emerged as the new
arbiters—and creators—of fine taste.

Styles come and go but the wedding ring has always been in
fashion. By the middle of the nineteenth century, posy rings, gimmel

A matching wedding ring and engagement ring set, Lucida®, by Tiffany & **o**
Company. The diamonds are cut in a classic yet contemporary cut, to show
the best advantage of the stone. The small stones on the wedding ring
match the shape of the diamond on the larger ring; Tiffany & Co.
Lucida® prong set and bezel set rings © Stephen Lewis.

rings, and the hand and heart designs were considered too frivolous to represent the sanctity of marriage. In New York in the late 1840s, according to an etiquette book of the time, large and ornate rings were not considered tasteful. A wedding ring, it was said, should be plain and made of gold. Tiffany told couples that their standard for wedding rings was 22-karat gold. The superb shaping and finishing of this luxurious metal transformed the so-called "plain" gold wedding ring into a bright, shiny, and colorful sight to behold.

A wedding band formed of multiple cables of precious metal twisted and held together with gems was the imaginative and lyrical design of French designer Jean Schlumberger of Tiffany. One of the twentieth century's most influential jewelry designers, Schlumberger's designs are still available at Tiffany & Company today.

The 1961 movie, *Breakfast at Tiffany's*, made Tiffany even more famous and forever linked rings and diamonds with romance and love. Tiffany designed and created a collection of wedding jewelry in the 1990s called Etoile®, which became popular with brides immediately. Receiving a ring in the famous blue box is the fantasy of many brides.

Just the two of us

INSCRIPTION

John Loring designed Tiffany's Atlas collection, introduced in 1995. It is based on the mythical tale of Atlas holding the world on his shoulders. The wedding rings feature crisp double bands and Roman numerals resembling those on a clock, with contrasting matte and polished surfaces. For couples of the late twentieth century, in love and always wanting more time together, these wedding rings said it all.

A wedding ring and matching engagement ring named Lucida®, for the brightest star in the constellation, was introduced by Tiffany in 1999. The diamond was cut in an entirely new way—classic yet contemporary. Small stones on the wedding ring match the shape of the engagement ring's larger stone. Gorgeous and desirable, the Lucida® set has found a permanent place in the hearts of women in love.

The famous Trinity Ring created by Cartier in 1918 is composed of three intertwined hoops in pink gold for love, white gold for friendship, and yellow gold for fidelity. The ring was specially created by Cartier for Jean Cocteau, the famous French poet, writer, artist and filmmaker as his token of love to his very intimate friend, the poet Raymond Radiguest. An immediate success, the Trinity Ring has endured throughout the years and today is a classic Cartier symbol of love and friendship. It has been worn as a wedding ring by British royals since its first appearance and is regarded as a traditional wedding ring in France.

The security and prosperity of the 1950s renewed the love of lavish designs in jewelry. Celebrity brides from the worlds of theater, movies, and high finance proudly wore the outstanding creations designed by famous jewelry houses like Tiffany & Company, Cartier, Harry Winston, Van Cleef & Arpels, and by Italian designers Bulgari and Bucellati. Their dazzling designer pieces were featured in movies and on the red carpet at the Academy Awards ceremonies. In the age of celebrity, the jewelers and their jewels also became stars.

Harry Winston, one of the world's most renowned jewelers, created the most fabulous jewelry for men who desired the best gifts for their lovers and wives. His name is still associated with the largest diamonds available to brides who appreciate the monetary value but who also respond to the deep emotional commitment those gems represent, with the fire and beauty shining beneath their frosty coating.

One of the most famous diamonds of all time is the Krupp-diamond, an Ascher-cut masterpiece weighing approximately 33 carats. This fine diamond, mounted in platinum with tapered baguette-cut diamond shoulders, is from the collection of Vera Krupp, originally from

top
Platinum wedding ring set
with 2.40 carats of baguette
cut diamonds; Harry Winston.
A signature wedding ring
crafted by world's most
renowned jewelry house.

bottom
A platinum wedding ring
of baguette cut diamonds
bar-set with round brilliant
cut diamonds, total weight of
diamonds 3.00 carats; Harry
Winston.

opposite
An emerald-cut diamond ring
weighing 5.40 carats set in
platinum with trapezoid cut
side stones; Harry Winston.
The jewelry house of Harry
Winston is associated with
the largest and the finest
diamonds available.

I love thee to the depth
and breadth and height
my soul can reach.

ELIZABETH BARRETT
BROWNING

Harry Winston. It was purchased by Richard Burton for Elizabeth Taylor in 1968. The ring only intensified the public's interest in the relationship of the two famous actors, making it—and them—legendary in the hearts of all who dream of such romance. Even when the couple parted some years later, the ring remained a symbol of passion.

The House of Bulgari, based in Rome, interprets jewelry through the Italian tradition that originated in the fifteenth century. Italian Renaissance jewelry was dominated by the use of color in dazzling and original ways, a design principle that is the trademark of the House of Bulgari today. Interpreting the workmanship of ancient Rome in a contemporary style, Bulgari is virtually the only jewelry house to join the ranks of Tiffany & Company, Cartier, and Harry Winston since World War II, and it is one of the world's most influential contemporary jewelers.

Hollywood played a key role in the twentieth century in romantically linking jewelry and love. When a man pledged his love to a woman with a diamond ring, audiences were thrilled. Jewelers collaborated with movie producers to show jewelry at its brightest. A diamond ring, whether large or small, was a big star as the ultimate symbol of eternal love, promised and given.

○ The Italian jewelry house of Bulgari in Rome, is often associated with the use of color in dazzling and original ways. Here the platinum diamond engagement ring and platinum wedding set interpret classical Renaissance jewelry in a contemporary way.

GONE BUT NOT FORGOTTEN

The sight of this, deserves a kiss.

<small>INSCRIPTION</small>

IN ENGLAND, DURING THE COMMONWEALTH 1649–1659, the Puritans tried to end the use of wedding rings because they regarded them as too ornate. While they were able to prohibit the use of wedding rings among themselves, ring-wearing women and gold-smiths raised an indignant protest. Soon the clergy ruled on the matter and decided that without a ring, a marriage could not be legal. Puritans in the American colonies felt wedding rings were frivolous, so brides and grooms exchanged thimbles instead. But often, after the wedding, the bottoms of the thimbles were cut off to create rings. The romance and emotion of the wedding ring was too firmly

This pearl and diamond ring dates from around 1890. Diamonds were used ○ either as solitaires or combined with pearls and used as betrothal rings among European couples. A treasured heirloom such as this provides insight into fashions and tastes of the past.

established in the minds and hearts of most people and the official ban never took place—since even an altered thimble was a ring.

The new colonists of Virginia and New York embraced the idea of the wedding ring. Stylish women in New York wore simple bands with ring guards, called keepers, containing small diamonds known as sparks. Another variation was the keeper ring or hoop ring, a diamond hoop of the Colonial period similar to today's wedding ring. Given for the betrothal, it was worn after the marriage next to the plain wide wedding band to prevent the band from being lost. Soon it became known as the guard ring. It was considered very bad luck to lose a wedding ring. Once placed on the finger by a clergyman, the ring was intended to stay on the finger for life.

The placement of rings on the finger in eighteenth-century Europe was a language all its own. A woman wearing a ring on the little finger was conveying the thought, "No marriage for me." The same ring worn on the index finger meant, "I am looking around." Women who were

o Wide gold band, traditional for southern Tyrol, an autonomous region of Italy near Austria. The ring is inscribed with the date of the wedding, "26 ten July 1819" and decorated in a scroll-like style with flowers and leaves. South Tyrol, 1819. The Alice and Louis Koch Collection

already married wore the ring on their middle finger. On the ring finger, betrothal was indicated.

HOW TO PROMOTE AND
SECURE HAPPINESS
IN THE MARRIED STATE

Always wear your wedding
ring for therein lies more
virtue than is usually
imagined. If you ruffled
unawares, assaulted with
improper thoughts, or
tempted in any kind
against your duty, cast
your eye upon it and call
to mind who gave it to you,
where it was received
and what passed at the
solemn time

LADY'S MONTHLY
MUSEUM, 1799

○

When Sonny and Cher got married in the early 1960s, they bought two stainless steel rings. Cher's was engraved "Sonny" and Sonny's was engraved "Cher." But Cher lost her ring in the couple's Bel Air, California, home soon after the wedding. In 1977, long after Sonny and Cher moved out, the Bel Air home was being remodeled and a construction worker found the ring in a demolition dumpster on the property. He didn't connect the inscription with Cher—until he saw Sonny and Cher singing together on *The Late Show with David Letterman* in the late 1990s. Cher mentioned she had lost her wedding ring years earlier and the construction worker contacted her and gave it back.

A New York newspaper reported that when a bridegroom could not find the wedding ring he had brought to the church, he desperately tore the ring from the rope across a pew and gave it to his bride. It was, of course, much too big for her finger. Still, the minister accepted it as a wedding ring.

"I've lost my wedding ring!"

When a woman's wedding ring fell into the river Clyde in Scotland, her husband accused her of giving it to a lover. He was so jealous he threatened her life. The woman went to the Bishop of Glasgow, and begged him to help her prove her faithfulness. So the compassionate bishop prayed for the ring to be found. A few hours later, a fisherman gave the Bishop a large salmon he had just caught in the river. In the salmon's mouth was the woman's lost wedding ring! Her husband vowed to be kind to his wife forevermore. The coat of arms of the city of Glasgow contains a picture of a salmon with a wedding ring in its mouth.

After John F. Kennedy was assassinated, Jackie stood by his coffin. She wanted to give him something to take with him on his last journey so she slipped her wedding ring from her finger and placed it upon his. But a while later she expressed her doubts to the couple's dear friend about what she'd done, saying, "Now I have nothing left." Her friend, Kenny O'Donnell, went to the hospital later that night and retrieved the ring. Jacqueline put the wedding ring back on her own finger.

When a New York writer was presented by her husband with an old, beautifully engraved gold wedding ring with flowers that was passed on from his grandmother, she felt welcomed and touched by his love and trust. Several years later, fearing she would lose it while on a vacation to the Caribbean, they decided to leave the ring at home.

Stick to me, my darling

INSCRIPTION ON A
TWENTIETH-CENTURY
WEDDING RING

Crazy for You

INSCRIPTION

While they were away, their apartment was robbed and the ring stolen. Both of them felt tremendous sadness in losing such a precious, irreplaceable jewel. Several months later, her husband found a similar ring in a small Greenwich Village jewelry shop and surprised her with it. Until today it remains on her finger, never to be taken off again.

Platinum three-row channel set wedding ring with narrow long baguette ⦿ diamonds between two rows of round diamonds. A special wedding ring can be worn alone without a diamond solitaire.

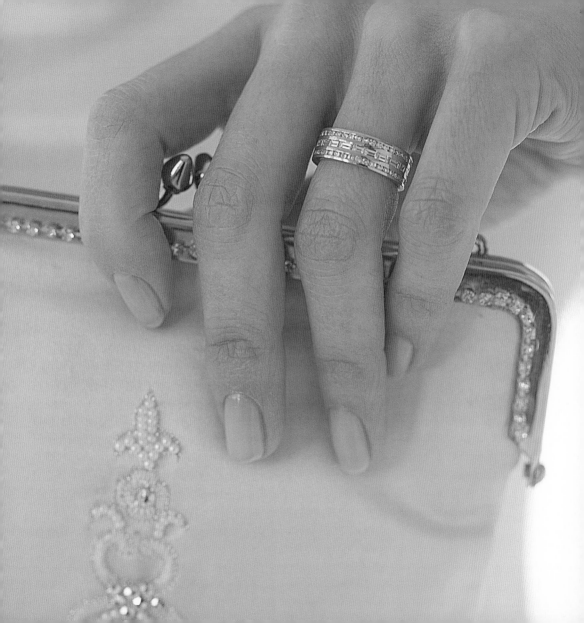

PRECIOUS METALS

I prize thy love more than whole mines of gold,
Or all the riches that the East doth hold,
My love is such that rivers cannot quench...

ANNE BRADSTREET, *TO MY DEAR AND LOVING HUSBAND*

ALTHOUGH THE FIRST RINGS WERE MADE OF A VARIETY OF braided grasses, over time, gold, bone, brass, iron, copper, jade, silver, and platinum were also used. The form of the ring, the endless circle, remains the same no matter what it's made of.

Celts in 100 B.C. in Western Europe wore iron jewelry as did Anglo Saxons in Britain during the Roman occupation. Rings of iron, copper, and brass were worn by the Greeks and Romans. Brass, however, was considered a "pretender to the throne" of finer metals and is still considered an inferior metal today. In fact, its presumptuousness in entering the field of finer metals has made the word a synonym for "impudence."

Texture and shape are the foundation of the Meringue Collection by O David Gomez, which is inspired by the magic of egg whites being whipped into clouds of confections.

A nugget of 22-carat Welsh yellow gold taken from Clogau Saint David's Mine was given to the Duke of York in 1923. A wedding ring was made from this remarkable treasure for his marriage to Lady Elizabeth Bowes-Lyon. Every royal wedding ring since the marriage of Princess Mary of Teck in 1893 has been made of this piece of Welsh gold. This same 22-carat gold nugget was used to create wedding rings for Princess Elizabeth in 1947, Princess Margaret in 1960, Princess Anne in 1973 and for Diana, the Princess of Wales, in 1981. In 1982 the British Legion presented a new bar of 22-carat Clogau Saint David's gold to the Queen. Sarah Ferguson wore the first ring made from this new nugget at her wedding to Prince Andrew in 1986.

Any groom contemplating whether to wear a wedding ring might be interested to know that Prince Albert, King Edward VII, and King George V all wore one on fourth finger of the left hand. In 1923, a new tradition was established by the royal gents: wearing a narrow

O Flowers inspired this ring by the designer Leila which combines various elements to give it depth and dimension. The beautiful yellow gold diamond flowers on white metal are part of a collection Leila created for OGI.

gold wedding ring on the little finger of the left hand, next to the gold signet ring.

The color of gold has been a symbol of royalty and riches throughout the ages, and it has been revered by millions of couples in love. It was the traditional metal used in wedding bands because it represents warmth and harmony and reminds us of the golden light of the sun.

But as beautiful as gold is, another metal has dazzled brides and grooms. Platinum, the rarest and most enduring of all metals, is the perfect symbol for a lifetime of love. Setting diamonds in platinum or another white metal displays the gems to their most dramatic effect. This idea first arose in the seventeenth century, when silver was used around rose diamonds in a piece of gold jewelry.

Platinum was brought to Europe for the first time in 1741 from Cartagena, Colombia. For a time, platinum was regarded as white gold. Resembling silver with its a silvery white appearance, platinum was called *platina del Pinto* by the Spaniards, *platina* being the diminutive of *plata* (silver) and Pinto the river in South America where the metal was first discovered. Platinum is often the metal of choice today for

It's unlucky to drop the ring on the floor during the wedding ceremony.

RING LORE

Diamonds set in gold, wrap around a plain band that was designed by Leila ○ for OGI to create a unique and contemporary ring.

both engagement and wedding rings because diamonds appear even more dazzling when set in platinum.

Platinum is so dense and durable that it can withstand a lifetime of constant wear. The pure, rare metal represents integrity and commitment. Many platinum wedding rings are perfectly plain, shining rounds that reflect the simple happiness and love a married couple shares. Some are engraved with symbols of peace, like a laurel wreath, or oak leaves representing strength. Ivy vines may also be used, to celebrate devotion that will never end.

The chic Parisians wear a diamond hoop wedding ring and a large solitaire diamond ring [in the evening]. By day an elegant woman would usually wear a wedding circlet of plain platinum.

HARPER'S BAZAAR, 1929

Yellow, green, pink, or white gold was the standard for wedding and engagement rings for centuries. Wedding rings that combined gold alloys with rose and yellow gold were also popular. But during World War II, because platinum and silver were needed for processing and manufacturing weapons and medical instruments, engagement and wedding rings could only be made of gold. When the alloys that go into gold were eventually needed, the government tried to cut back on the use of gold in jewelry. At the same time, there was a sharp rise in the demand for wedding rings. In fact, the number of wedding rings being

ring quality

When purchasing your wedding rings, make sure you are getting the quality you are paying for. A fine ring will have its manufacturer's trademark stamped upon it as well as the karat content of the ring. Regulations on the marking of gold jewelry go back to the days when gold and other metals were used as money and the penalties for violating them were severe. Today, in the United States, omitting a quality mark on a ring is not a violation of law, but every purchaser of a wedding ring should look for a quality mark followed by a registered trademark.

Quality marks for platinum differ by country. Rings at least ninety-five percent pure are stamped "platinum" or "plat" in the United States. PT950 or 950 PT in Europe, Platine in Canada.

- The platinum purity makes the ring hypoallergenic.
- The surface will scratch just like any other metal but it will not dent as deeply.
- In the United States, the purity of gold is designated by karat, pure gold is 24k,
  but, because of its softness, it is not suitable for making jewelry.
- In Europe, gold is stamped according to its fineness. Pure gold is really 100% pure;
  18k is seventy-five percent or 750 fine and 14k is fifty-eight and one third percent fine.

purchased exceeded the number of weddings. The war inspired brides and grooms to revive the old-fashioned custom of their European grandparents—the double ring ceremony. This explained the rise in demand for gold wedding rings. New husbands, the men who were preparing to possibly sacrifice their lives abroad, wanted to carry with them a symbol of home and family. Their brides wanted the double ring

ceremony for another reason. Their soldier husbands would have a tangible symbol to help them remember—and proclaim—their marital status.

At the height of the war in 1943, eighty percent of marrying couples used two rings at their wedding, compared with an average of less than fifteen percent of couples in 1940, the year before the United States joined the war. By the end of 1944 the proportion of double-ring ceremonies was ninety-four percent of the total. The United States government stepped in and lifted the curb on gold for wedding rings. Not even the industrial needs of a nation at war could be permitted to interfere with the wedding ring.

The purity of marriage deserves to be celebrated with pure metals. If gold or platinum is not used in a wedding ring, silver is acceptable. But copper, brass and other metals that may corrode are not recommended because they can stain the skin.

The special virtue of a gold wedding ring is so important in some parts of Ireland that a bridegroom will rent a ring for his wedding if he cannot afford to buy one. Often, the justice of the peace keeps a gold

(*continued on page 108*)

○ Gumit's Karu infinity ring is derived from the Yoni Symbol, which is the woman's fertility symbol in the Hindu tradition. Gumit created the symbol in gold and studded it with a diamond then interlocked the pieces to create the band.

ring settings

Each ring setting has its own personality.

PRONG it is invisible from all sides for maximum sparkle

CHANNEL stones are set between two parallels of metal

BAR features a thin metal bar that separates each stone

PAVE tiny metal beads hold each stone

TENSION setting grips the stone with 65-95 pounds of pressure, creating the illusion that stone is hovering in space

FLUSH offers the security of small stones inside the holes

prong   channel   bar   pave   tension   flush

If you don't choose to have a stone set, you have a multitude of options for a ○ wedding ring. Here a white gold ring has tiny spheres that are meant to create tingling music when the ring moves. A yellow gold ring, inspired by one from Ethopia, has little hoops meant to look like fields of flowers. Both were crafted by Alessandra Ravenna of Rome.

ring available to lend to couples. In Yorkshire, England, some people say that marrying with a borrowed ring brings good luck.

But any material may be used if either of the spouses has handmade the wedding ring, because the act of crafting a ring for one's future spouse is more precious than any metal. If a handmade ring cannot be worn on the finger, it can be worn on a chain around the neck.

Matching wedding rings for the bride and the groom became popular in the 1970s. Although some of the wedding rings were diamond-studded, most couples chose traditional gold bands. Twentieth-century men often preferred gold to platinum. Today, most couples choose double ring ceremonies, and many magnificent designs are available to both the bride and groom. Wedding sets, for example, consist of a wedding ring that complements the woman's engagement ring and also offer a matching band for the groom. That's why it's important to think about your wedding ring when selecting your engagement ring.

○ A gold wedding ring contains inscriptions inside the hoop in Korean and English along with a message that contains a heart, a symbol that is universal.

Platinum wedding rings hand engraved with "miniature nature" designs are created ○ today by Alex Pugachevski for OGI. The art of engraving on precious metal and stones started during the 4th century B.C. in Mesopotamia. The surface of the metal is decorated by incising pictures with a sharply pointed steel tool. The engraver may even use a microscope to define the details of the designs.

Though many men say they don't feel comfortable wearing rings, seventy-five percent of them are romantic enough to wear a wedding ring that matches the metal of the ring of their spouse. Men do enjoy inscriptions on their wedding rings, either the date of the wedding, their first date, or perhaps her pet name and a private message they share.

It is fun and often easy to come up with the inscriptions you and your mate will have in your wedding rings to commemorate your commitment to one another. But actually engraving your carefully chosen words, letters, and images on your rings is a skill few people possess.

The engraving and carving of jewelry started during the fourth century B.C., in Mesopotamia, during the Elamite and Sumerian civilizations. The Greeks and Romans raised jewelry engraving to such heights that it has been said they provide a "miniature history" of art. Florentine and German engravers revived the art of engraving by the end of the fourteenth century. Renaissance artists co-opted the designs of Greek and Roman times with a freedom of interpretation that made their work unique.

Hand engraving is done in much the same way today as it was centuries ago. The surface of the metal is decorated by incising letters or pictures with a sharply pointed steel tool, called a scupper, while the metal is held on an engraver's block. The engraver may even use a microscope to define the details of the design. The additional skill of calligraphy is required when engraving monograms or inscriptions.

Some men are setting a new trend in the twenty-first century by choosing rings made of titanium, a metallic element with the strength of steel but the weight of aluminum. Titanium wedding rings come in silvery-gray or black, but can feature color accents or even be specially made in a variety of colors. Diamonds can also be set in titanium rings for extra luxury and luster. For those whose jobs or activities would cause heavy wear and tear on jewelry, the strength and durability of titanium is a wise choice. The name refers to the strength of the race of the mythological Greek Titans.

All sorts of metals are strong and shimmering, but they cannot compare to the magnetic attraction that draws two people together to forge a union of love, commitment, and family. The real circle of love is the one made by a couple in one another's arms.

FULL-CIRCLE: ARTIST-JEWELERS

I am my beloved's and my beloved is mine.

SOLOMON'S SONG OF SONGS

SINCE THE 1960S, THE DESIGN AND MANUFACTURE OF THE wedding ring has changed dramatically, bringing new techniques and materials that enhance the beauty and durability of the timeless circle of love. Modern jewelry designers are creating wedding rings based on geometrical construction and on contemporary discoveries while retaining the classic form. The designs vary with the diversity of sources of inspiration, but they continue to evoke the spiritual, universal and timeless emotions of love. Regardless of the material or the design, whether classically simple or dazzlingly lavish, the most

Golden scales ring with cabochon rubies by Ralph Bakker, ⊙
a jewelry-artist, whose work is inspired by Benvenuto Cellini,
a Renaissance era sculptor and goldsmith

○ Purity in form and an industrial aesthetic are the hallmarks of William Richey's designs, which combine platinum with yellow, pink, and white gold.

important aspect of the wedding ring has remained the same: the delicate, breathtaking and universal love between partners that it always has, and always will, represent.

The innovative designs of today's jewelry artists take the wedding ring to new heights that dazzle the eye, engage the mind, and, of course, continue to touch the heart. Now more than ever before, the wedding ring is a statement of the emotional bond between the artists, their materials and the couple who selects, and often participates in, the design of the ring.

Even more significant than the new design concepts in rings is the change in the relationship between future husbands and wives. In the decades following the 1960s, women's roles changed dramatically. Now the small circular band contains new dreams, ideas, and beliefs— the marriage as a partnership between equals, two strong individuals embarking on a path of love and life together. The couple and the artist-jeweler come together to bring their individual and collective visions of love and marriage to life. The precious wedding ring is an expression of their combined and equal creativity, a link between one person's artistic interpretation and the couple's vision of their love.

O The international star designer Steve Midgett works with Mokume Gane, an ancient Japanese metal-working technique developed in Feudal Japan. Layers of contrasting colored metal are fusion welded together by high heat and pressure. The resulting material is then manipulated by forging, twisting and carving to develop more complex patterns.

The twenty-first century is about making individual choices based on personal interpretation of the circle of love, whether returning to timeless antiques or employing cutting-edge artistry. From museums to independent galleries to department stores, from freestanding retail shops to your local mom and pop jewelers to the internet's e-commerce stores, today's creativity in wedding rings is enchanting.

Fine art and highly specialized manufacturing techniques come together in the wedding and engagement rings of the German firm, Niessing. The innovative partnership the company pursues with artist-jewelers results in fabulous rings offered in limited editions. One of the best-known Niessing designs is the tension ring, in which two rounded hoops of metal hold stones that appear to be suspended in air—love in all its glory is like a star floating in the sky. The stone, floating freely in its setting, invokes the beauty of love freely given and received. Designed by Ursula Exner the ring is registered and protected by Niessing, but the idea of suspended stones has been used in other rings attempting to recreate a similar effect.

O The diamond appears to be floating in this tension set diamond ring designed by Ursula Exner for Niessing. The innovative partnership Niessing pursues with artist-jewelers results in fabulous rings offered in limited editions.

A ring crowned with pearls was crafted by Rainer Milewski of Germany. Since the O 1960s, artist jewelers have been inspired by nature and history. The emotional bond between the artists and their followers allow jewelry to be worn as art.

The delicate jewelry designs of Ted Muehling, whose workshop and jewelry boutique are in Manhattan's Soho district, celebrate the natural world. His admiration of seashells and eggshells inspire the shapes and lines of his wedding rings. For the couple enamored of nature (as well as of each other) these wedding rings symbolize a connection to nature that is as timeless as love itself.

While many couples embark into new territory in the design of their wedding rings, classic and traditional wedding rings are still very much in demand. Isn't it interesting that no matter how quickly we march into the future, most of us prefer to celebrate eternal love with a wedding ring that represents the history of that emotion? Perhaps the appeal of these classic styles is that they connect us to our parents and grandparents as we continue to look forward to new generations and the continuation of our families. Such traditional designs reinforce our desire for balance and harmony in everyday life and strengthen our spiritual connection with nature.

O The delicate jewelry designs of Ted Muehling of New York celebrate the natural world. The yellow gold "his and hers" wedding rings are inspired by the shapes and line of seashells and eggshells.

This is a modern version of an old Jewish wedding ring by Swed Masters Workshops. The O new rendition is decorated with filigree and domed to display a temple, which can be worn separately as a pendant after the wedding. The ring inside can be worn as a wedding ring.

Many brides seem to prefer a wedding ring with the most traditional techniques, forms and historic references. With these rings couples reaffirm the sacramental value of their commitment to each other, especially when they exchange rings in religious wedding ceremonies.

A modern version of the old Jewish wedding ring with its elaborate architectural features is crafted by Swed Masters Workshop, in Jerusalem. Centuries ago, this type of ring was slipped onto the right index finger of the bride and then kept not by her, but by her family or her congregation. The new rendition is decorated with filigree all around and domed to display a temple or a home. It follows the spiritual tradition of the Jewish faith and makes the most of the technical and aesthetic qualities of the metal and the skill of the crafters. Now the bride can wear the ring after the ceremony.

On these pages are a selection of many artist-jewelers working today. Their unique designs allow couples to choose rings that make a statement and truly reflect their personal style.

20-carat gold wrap rings for the bride and plain for the groom were created **o**
by Susanne Miller of Germany. The wrap rings echo the dreams and hopes
wrapping around the body and soul of two people combining a life together.

HAPPILY EVER AFTER

How do I love thee, let me count the ways.

ELIZABETH BARRETT BROWNING

TO MAKE SURE YOU HAVE YOUR BANDS IN PLENTY OF TIME for the big day, know that they should be ordered four months before the wedding date and picked up six weeks before. Just remember to keep them in a safe place (one that you'll remember) until the ceremony.

Before you order your rings though, you want to make sure that they'll fit for a lifetime. The wedding ring must be tight enough that you don't worry about losing it—but also loose enough to fit your finger for all the years that you wear it. We are all sentimental about our wedding rings, and some of us are superstitious about ever removing them once they've been placed on our fingers by our cherished mates.

The dream of every bride and groom starting their lives together is to live ○ happily ever after. The blue box from Tiffany & Co. has become a cultural signifier of romance; The Tiffany ® setting, © Carlton Davis.

Be realistic—your finger may become a bit plumper over the years. Plan now for your wedding ring to be comfortable for the rest of your life. But don't worry: if your ring becomes impossible to wear, it is acceptable to wear it on a chain around your neck. This is considered equivalent to wearing it on the finger. It's also possible to get the ring enlarged if necessary.

After you've gotten the right fit you might start to think of ways to be sure your spouse won't temporarily remove the wedding ring. Consider a puzzle ring, often used as men's wedding rings in Greece and Italy. The puzzle ring is composed of many interlocking bands that must be arranged in a particular way to form a single ring. Few people can put it back together quickly once it is removed from the finger. A contemporary option is a ring with movable needles so the ring is easy to slip on but nearly impossible to remove.

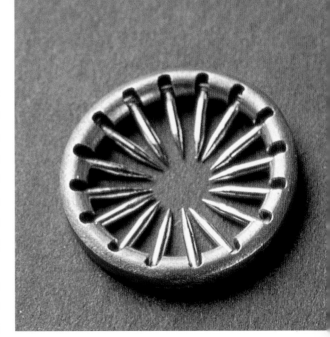

○ Gold wedding "torture ring" by Ralph Bakker who explains that "the needles on the inside are moveable—it is easy to put the ring on and they are very wearable. But when you try to lay them aside, you have to be very careful." Photo: Derk-Jan Wooldrik.

cleaning your wedding ring

The key word is gentle. You don't want to damage your beautiful ring with harsh cleansers. If your stones are cracked or loose in their settings, have them repaired or tightened by your jeweler—do not try to clean them yourself.

Use a little detergent in warm water or a mixture of half cold water and half household ammonia. Let the ring soak for 30 minutes. Remove the ring and use a small, soft new toothbrush to gently clean around the front and back of the mounting. Swish the ring again in the solution and allow it to dry on a paper or cloth towel. A little polish with a soft chamois will thoroughly restore the brilliancy of the stone.

I love you for the part of me that you bring out.

ANONYMOUS

Each year, your wedding anniversary gives you a chance to rediscover the bonds that drew you and your loving mate together, to re-affirm why you chose to marry one another. Your wedding anniversary symbolizes the continuing commitment you have to one another. What better way to celebrate than with an anniversary ring? Anniversary rings are usually designed with a series of small diamonds or colored gemstones that go around the entire ring. They are beautiful symbols of love without end. You may select your anniversary ring to match or complement your wedding and engagement rings or you may choose a fresh, new design to proclaim the evolving nature of your lifelong love.

These two wedding rings are set with princess cut diamonds. The special ○ cut was invented in the late 20th century and immediately became popular. Brides often chose their center stone engagement ring in this same cut. The diamonds are cut in a square shape on top and brilliant cut on the back to create more sparkle and light.

Other anniversary customs include the Japanese tradition of every ten years a husband gives his wife a diamond ring to mark their wedding anniversary. The Chinese believe that life has four major milestones worth celebrating: birth, coming of age, the wedding, and anniversaries.

The wedding ring will always be a symbol of the union between two people in love. We feel naked without it. We never take it off and we remain protected and loved within its beautiful circle. A perfect, divine form that joins two hearts in eternal love, the wedding ring is a sign of strength and power. But the real value of the wedding ring has always been and will always be measured in moments, days and years of devotion shared by two people in love.

From the very rich to the very humble, from the biggest stars to ordinary people, lovers continue to celebrate the magic they find encircled in one another's arms by wearing the most precious circle of all—the wedding ring. In every country in the world, each couple that exchanges rings adds another unique chapter to the long history of betrothal and pledge rings, engagement, and wedding rings.

May this marriage be full of laughter, our every day in paradise.

May this marriage be a sign of compassion, a seal of happiness here and hereafter.

RUMI,
THIS MARRIAGE—ODE 2667

O Matching wedding bands in platinum are often chosen for their beautiful simplicity and as symbols of hope, fidelity, and commitment to family and future.

celebrate your years together

YEAR 1   a platinum wedding ring with small diamonds totaling one carat

YEAR 10   a platinum sapphire and diamond band to wear with your original wedding ring

YEAR 25   platinum diamond ring totaling five carats to celebrate the silver anniversary

YEAR 50   renewal of marriage vows with a new platinum band

The most endearing human qualities—hope and fidelity, commitment to family and future—are enveloped in the wedding ring. The world always changes, but the wedding ring remains the token of love that not only unites two people in the present, but also unites all who believe in love for eternity. Each time we look at the third finger of the left hand and see the wedding ring, the love that drew us to our beloved shines even more brightly than the precious metal and sparkles even more than the finest diamond. It reminds us of the dream of love eternal, the dream that came true.

Ajour rings by Carla Nuis are a series of nine different designs based on sixteenth- and seventeenth-century ornamental patterns. Nuis is an established Dutch designer who is represented in renowned craft galleries throughout the world. Her work has been included in various public collections, including that of the Victoria and Albert Museum in London. Photo: Eddy Wenting.

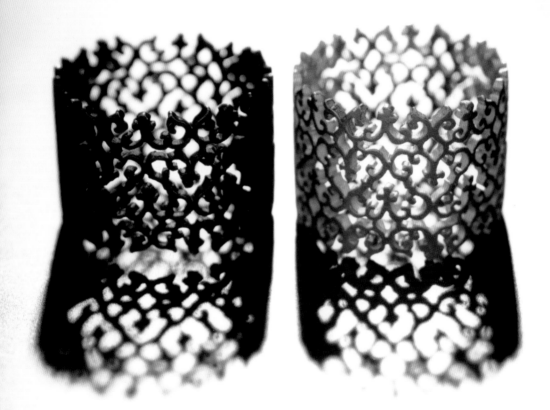

ACKNOWLEDGMENTS

Many thanks to my close friends and family for their belief in this project and their encouragement to pursue it. To Larry for his guidance and constant verification of historical events. To Bill Lucky for giving me the time and the support to write the book. To Anne Baker for her research assistance. To Lisa, Ala, Thwe, Irina, and Isaac whose support and spirit navigated me through the making of this book. And a special thank you to Jo Sgammato and Beth Huseman for their patience and help in juggling the many changes.

I would also like to thank all the jewelry designers and the jewelry houses for their support and commitment through this project.

CREDITS

Thanks to the following for providing props for new photography or for furnishing their own images: Ralph Bakker, Netherlands; The British Museum, London; Bulgari, Italy; Cartier, New York; Charon Kransen, New York; David Gomez, New York; Furrer Jacot, USA; Gurmit Designs, New York; Harry Winston, USA; Bill Helin, USA; Jytte Klove, Denmark; The Alice and Louis Koch Collection, Switzerland; Steve Midgett, USA; Rainer Milewski, Germany; Susanne Miller, Germany; Ted Muehling, New York; Nelson D' Leon (bridal headpiece designer) New York; Niessing North America, USA; John C. Nordt, USA; Carla Nuis, Netherlands; Alessandra Ravenna, Italy; Rawat Gems, New York; Réunion des Musées Nationaux, Paris; Robert Simon, New York; Bruce Smith Ltd., New York; Spectore Titanium, USA; Swed Masters Workshop, Israel; Takohl Design, Chicago; Tiffany & Co., USA; True Romance®, New York; Hubert Verstraeten, Belgium; Victoria & Albert Museum, London; William Richey, USA

SOURCES

Baldizzone, Gianni, and Tiziana Baldizzone. *Wedding Ceremonies*. Paris: Flammarion, 2001

Dickinson, Joan Y. *The Book of Diamonds*. New York: Dover, 2001

Gandy Fales, Martha. *Jewelry in America 1600–1900*. New York: Antique Collectors' Club, 1988

Johns, Catherine. *The Jewelery of Roman Britain*. Ann Arbor: University of Michigan Press, 1996

Kunz, George Frederick. *Rings for the Finger*. New York: Dover, 1917

Lambert, Sylvie. *The Ring*. Switzerland: RotoVision SA, 1998

Lys, Claudia de. *How the World Weds*. New York: Martin Press, 1929

Matlins, A.L. and A. Bonanno. *Engagement & Wedding Rings*. Vermont: Gemstone Press, 1999

Mullins, Kathy and Bride's Magazine. *Bride's Little Book of Vows and Rings*. New York: Random House, 1994

Munn, Geoffrey C. *The Triumph of Love*. New York: Thames and Hudson, 1993

Newman, Harold. *Illustrated Dictionary of Jewelry*. New York: Thames and Hudson, 1987

Oman, C.C. *Catalogue of Rings 1930*. London: Victoria and Albert Museum, 1993

Remington, James McCarthy. *Rings through the Ages*. New York: Harper & Brothers, 1817

Scarisbrick, Diana. *Rings*. New York: Abrams, 1993

Tait, Hugh., ed. *Jewelry 7,000 Years*. New York: Abrams, 1987

Taylor, Elizabeth. *My Love Affair with Jewelry*. New York: Simon & Schuster, 2002

Taylor, Gerald, and Diana Scarisbrick. *Finger Rings*. Oxford: Lund Humphries, 1978

And as this round

Is nowhere found

To flaw, or else to sever,

So let our love

As endless prove,

And pure as gold forever.

ROBERT HERRICK

Published in 2004 by
Stewart, Tabori & Chang
115 West 18th Street
New York, NY 10011

Canadian Distribution:
Canadian Manda Group
One Atlantic Avenue, Suite 105
Toronto, Ontario M6K 3E7
Canada

Cataloging-in-Publication Data is on file with the Library of Congress.
ISBN: 1-58479-375-9

Editor Beth Huseman
Designer Amy Trombat
Production Manager Jane Searle

The text of this book was composed in Fairfield and DIN

Printed in China
10 9 8 7 6 5 4 3 2 1
First Printing

Stewart, Tabori & Chang is a subsidiary of La Martinière Groupe

LA MARTINIÈRE

Photo page 141

This matching set of engagement and wedding ring created by one of the largest wedding ring manufacturers, True Romance®, is traditional and yet contemporary. The company's many designs employ the latest technology and expertise.